FOOD PYRAMID
Fats, Oils, and Sweets
Dairy
Meat
Veggies
Fruits
Grains

This book is dedicated to all the healthcare workers, the curious minds, and the aspiring dreamers. May you explore the world of endless possibilities, embrace your passions, and discover your strengths. May your journey through different careers be full of excitement and fulfillment.

MASCOT KIDS!
an imprint of Amplify Publishing Group

www.mascotbooks.com

What Can I Do? Healthcare Edition

For more information, please contact:
Mascot Kids, an imprint of Amplify Publishing Group
620 Herndon Parkway, Suite 220
Herndon, VA 20170
info@mascotbooks.com

Library of Congress Control Number: 2025915116

CPSIA Code: PRKF0925A

ISBN-13: 979-8-89138-661-7

Printed in China

What Can I Do?

Healthcare Edition

by KEVIN HAYES

illustrated by RACHEL NOVEL

WHAT CAN I DO?

Welcome to *What Can I Do? Healthcare Edition*!

In this book, we will explore all sorts of different healthcare careers people can have. From dentists to nurses and therapists to paramedics, there are so many exciting and interesting jobs to learn about.

Let's get started!

Optometrists are eye doctors who help people see clearly. They check vision, look for any eye health problems, and prescribe glasses and contacts. They work in clinics and help people see the world . . .

but what can I do? I still don't have a clue!

Dentists are doctors for teeth! They help keep teeth and gums healthy, fix cavities, and teach us how to brush and floss. Dentists make sure our smiles are healthy and bright . . .

but what can I do? I still don't have a clue!

Nurse practitioners are advanced nurses who can diagnose illnesses, prescribe medicine, and provide treatment. They work in clinics and hospitals, helping people feel better . . .

but what can I do? I still don't have a clue!

Psychiatrists are similar to psychologists. They both help people with their mental health by talking with them, but psychiatrists are doctors who help people with medicine. They work to help people feel happy and healthy inside . . .

but what can I do? I still don't have a clue!

Psychologists help people understand their thoughts and feelings. They talk with people about their problems and teach them ways to feel better. They work in hospitals, schools, and private offices . . .

but what can I do? I still don't have a clue!

Surgeons are doctors who perform operations to fix problems inside the body, using special tools. Surgeons are often found in hospitals and operating rooms . . .

but what can I do? I still don't have a clue!

Physician assistants work closely with doctors to examine patients, prescribe treatments, and assist in surgeries. They help patients feel comfortable and get better . . .

but what can I do? I still don't have a clue!

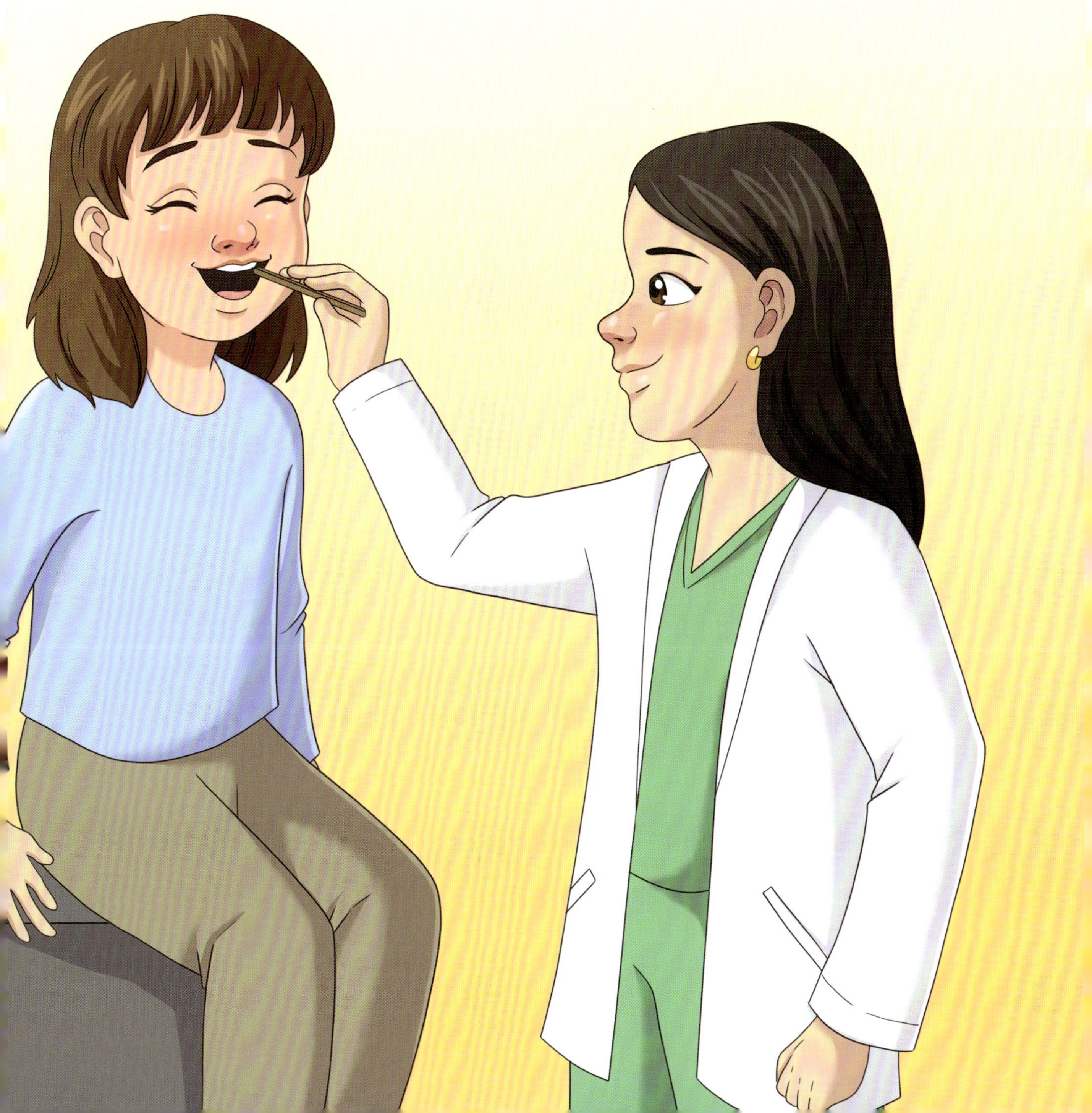

Dietitians teach people how to eat healthy to stay strong and energized. They create meal plans and give advice on nutritious foods that make people feel their best . . .

but what can I do? I still don't have a clue!

Paramedics are emergency responders who help people during accidents or health emergencies. They work in ambulances, providing first aid and taking people to the hospital . . .

but what can I do? I still don't have a clue!

Pharmacists help people get the right medicines. They work in pharmacies, hospitals, and clinics, making sure everyone understands how to take their medicine safely . . .

but what can I do? I still don't have a clue!

Pharmacy technicians work with pharmacists to prepare medicines and help people at the pharmacy. They organize prescriptions and make sure patients get the right medication . . .

but what can I do? I still don't have a clue!

Surgical technicians work alongside surgeons during operations. They make sure everything is clean and ready in the operating room, set up tools, and help during surgery . . .

but what can I do? I still don't have a clue!

Laboratory technicians work with samples, like blood and tissue, to help doctors diagnose illnesses. They work in labs, using special equipment to find answers that will help patients . . .

but what can I do? I still don't have a clue!

Athletic trainers help athletes stay healthy and recover from injuries. They work at schools, gyms, and sports teams to help people stay in shape and avoid getting hurt . . .

but what can I do?
I still don't have a clue!

Healthcare administrators work to ensure that hospitals and clinics are managed properly. They supervise staff, organize schedules, and keep everything organized for doctors and nurses . . .

but what can I do?
I still don't have a clue!

Respiratory therapists help people breathe better. They work with patients who have breathing problems, using special machines and exercises to improve their lung health . . .

but what can I do? I still don't have a clue!

Occupational therapists help people do everyday activities after an injury or illness. They teach exercises and techniques to help people gain independence at home, school, or work . . .

but what can I do? I still don't have a clue!

Speech therapists help people communicate clearly. They work with children and adults who have trouble speaking, helping them practice sounds and build confidence . . .

but what can I do? I still don't have a clue!

Audiologists are specialists who help people hear better. They test hearing and provide hearing aids to make sounds clearer. They help people of all ages enjoy the sounds around them . . .

but what can I do? I still don't have a clue!

Anesthesiologists are doctors who give medicine to make patients sleep or feel comfortable during surgery. They stay with patients during their operations, carefully monitoring them using special equipment to keep them safe . . .

but what can I do?
I still don't have a clue!

Pathologists study tissues and cells to understand diseases. They help doctors diagnose health problems by examining samples under a microscope . . .

but what can I do? I still don't have a clue!

Radiologists are doctors who use imaging like X-rays and MRIs to see inside the body. They help diagnose problems and work with other doctors to decide the best treatment . . .

but what can I do? I still don't have a clue!

Radiography technicians help take X-rays and other scans to see inside the body. They work with patients, helping them stay comfortable during the imaging process . . .

but what can I do? I still don't have a clue!

Physical therapists help people recover from injuries and surgeries. They use special techniques and exercise to help people regain strength and mobility. They work in hospitals, clinics, and even people's homes . . .

but what can I do? I still don't have a clue!

Biomedical engineers create medical devices and equipment that improve patient care, like artificial limbs, pacemakers, and medical imaging machines. They combine engineering skills with medical knowledge to design solutions that help doctors and nurses take care of patients . . .

but what can I do? I still don't have a clue!

Social workers help people in need. They work with children and families to provide support and assistance in housing, financial aid, and mental health. They work in various settings, including hospitals, schools, and social service agencies . . .

but what can I do? I still don't have a clue!

When I grow up, what can I do?
There are so many paths—oh, it's true!
I can follow my heart, chase my dreams,
explore the world, and find my themes.

Could I be a doctor and help the sick?
Or maybe a builder with a hammer and brick?
Could I make movies or design the next game?
Or be a scientist with discoveries to claim?

Perhaps I'll write stories or sing a sweet song,
help animals heal, where they belong.
I might lead a team or teach in a school,
fix pipes, fly planes, or enforce the rules.

Each job is special, each job is great,
from farming our food to fixing a gate.
Whatever I choose, I'll do it with care,
because every career is needed everywhere.

The world is big, the choices are vast,
I'll find my way—step by step, not too fast.
With hard work and passion, there's nothing I can't do,
so, what about you—what will you choose to pursue?

No matter what career I choose, it's important to work hard and be passionate about what I do. With determination and dedication, I can achieve my dreams and make a difference in the world!

About the Author

Kevin Hayes is a father, entrepreneur, and retired Army professor. He is from Columbia, South Carolina, and he is based in San Antonio, Texas. Kevin is a technology consultant who holds advanced degrees and education in Computer Science and Business from the University of Maryland, Webster University, Texas A&M University, and Purdue University. Kevin has a passion for leading and developing the youth and loves helping others achieve their goals. The What Can I Do? Career Day Series was inspired by his family and friends to spark kids' interests early about the vast careers and opportunities in life.